SOUTHAMPTON

SOUTHAMPTON

ROSIE WINDSOR

The History Press

First published 2018

The History Press
The Mill, Brimscombe Port
Stroud, Gloucestershire, GL5 2QG
www.thehistorypress.co.uk

British Library Cataloguing in Publication Data.
A catalogue record for this book is available from the British Library.

ISBN 978 0 7509 8901 5

Typesetting and origination by The History Press
Printed in China

INTRODUCTION

We all live in the same world, inhabit the same space and move through places at the same time, but we all see something different. Our minds are full of the pressures of life: somewhere to be, someone to meet, so little time. We race by, ignoring the very things in front of us all the time: images, patterns, people, light and shade. For an artist, the environment we live in is an ever-changing canvas of inspiration.

Coming from a creative background of fine art and life drawing, the images that surround me fill me with wonder and energy, or sometimes comfort and reassurance. The need to share this view of the world led to a degree in photography and a career as a photojournalist for several years, supplying images of the world to the national press.

Street photography allows us to capture a moment in time; an observation from the world around us. So many people passing by, so few people to notice the world as it is. What is it that appeals to a street photographer? Something that just catches the eye. A reflection, a line, a colour, shadows? People caught in a moment; sometimes unaware, sometimes merging with the landscape to stand out, to make a visual statement. A moment of poignancy, banality or humour.

Look around you. Share the complexity of the world we live in. Catch those moments – the structures, the people, the ever-changing flux of movement, unique for that split second of time.

The images within this book reflect a small sample of life in the city of Southampton, the environment and the people moving through it. I hope it inspires you to look afresh at the spaces we live in. That you will stand back and take a moment to see what is largely invisible, but, actually, is there all the time.

FOREWORD

'God is in the Details' – this is the famous dictum of German architect Mies van der Rohe. It suggests to me great focus, perception and personal application: qualities required by the street photographer and found abundantly in the work of Rosie Windsor. If you enquire about a city you will be told of its buildings and landmarks, its historic town walls and port. But if you really want to understand the nature of a city and its people then that is found at street level in the details of the everyday.

In these pages Rosie has used the act of photographing to reveal the city to us one subtle fragment at a time. The pictures tell us about Southampton but they also tell us about modern British life as a whole, the shiny new retail developments with balconied apartments, the homogenisation of our high streets, the ubiquitous smartphones and the 'pop-up' shop. These are familiar pictures to any British person brought up in a regional town or city.

This is the life we have made for ourselves and the street photographer candidly reflects that in the mirror their pictures hold up to society. Making pictures of public life unobserved could be considered a subversive activity but the uncensored record it creates is crucial and very difficult to find anywhere else.

Rosies' photographic details of contemporary Southampton life will become a landmark in the city's cultural history.

Nick Turpin, 2018

Killing time at Guildhall Square

Above Bar Street framed by post boxes

Travelling past Argos at West Bargate

Following pages: Mobile phone generations on Commercial Road and West Bargate

'F*** it', New Road

Thieves fail to nab this bike at Bargate Street

West Bargate

Previous page: Castle Way

Photographing the photographer at Hanover Buildings

Opposite: Street fashion, Above Bar Street

Overleaf: Above Bar Street

Colour coordination at Harbour Parade

Leading the way along Above Bar Street

Loud wheels, Bargate Street

Just passing through, Portland Terrace

In profile, Hanover buildings

Shooting some hoops at Mayflower Park

Opposite: Forest View

Home furnishings, West Quay Shopping Centre

Opposite: Ikea, West Quay Road

Western Esplanade

Vital morning coffee fix, Caffè Nero, Above Bar Street

Safety first, Bedford Place

Overleaf: Bargate Street

Curved lines, Forest View

Civic Centre Road #urbanflowteam #parkour

Overleaf: Mayflower Park

Harbour Parade

Time for sunnies, Above Bar Street

Opposite: Keeping in lane, Harbour Parade

Overleaf: And relax. Bill's, Western Esplanade

West Quay

Above Bar Street

Playing ball, Mayflower Park

Opposite: Castle Way

Right: Above Bar Street

Overleaf: Ikea, West Quay Road

Right: One-man parade, Above Bar Street

Opposite: Bargate Street

Chit-chat, The Artisan, Guildhall Square

West Quay

Right: Bill's, Western Esplanade

Overleaf: Above Bar Street

Mayflower Park

Enjoying a spot of shopping, Civic Centre Road

West Quay

Opposite: Skateboarders dismount, Above Bar Street

While you wait, Above Bar Street

Western Esplanade

Take off, Civic Centre Road

Overleaf: Western Esplanade

Harbour Parade

Bargate Street

Opposite: West Quay

The anticipation of take off, Above Bar Street

Above Bar Street

Watching and waiting, Bargate Street

Overleaf: Harbour Parade

Right: A case of the giggles,
Western Esplanade

Overleaf: West Quay

Bernard Street

Opposite: Portland Terrace

The other side of the glass, Turtle Bay, Above Bar Street

Queue for ink, Bedford Place

Right and overleaf: Beatnik
Emporium, Above Bar Street

West Quay maze, Western Esplanade

Overleaf: West Quay Shopping Centre, Harbour Parade

From above, West Quay Shopping Centre, Harbour Parade

'Love your record collection', Vinilo Records, Queensway

There's always time for a chin wag, The Art House Café, Above Bar Street

Opposite : A novel mode of transport, Above Bar Street

Overleaf: Above Bar Street

Above Bar Street

Above Bar Street

The fairground awaits, Above Bar Street

The Bin Trail, artist Kev Mundy / Stand Together, Above Bar Street

Hot Hot Hot, Turtle Bay, Above Bar Street

Turtle Bay, Above Bar Street

Opposite: Civic Centre Road

Above: The Artisan, Guildhall Square

Overleaf: Sixteen Exhibition, Southampton Solent University, Guildhall Square